THE WEIRD AND WONDERFUL WORLD OF ACCOUNTANCY

By Marvin Close

With Holly Close

INTRODUCTION

Accountants boring? You must be joking. As this book will reveal, they've been at the heart of some of civilisation's most amazing inventions, advances and events.

We're going to look at how accountancy was instrumental in the creation of Led Zeppelin and the invention of bubble gum. How the power of the accountant's pen put gangster Al Capone behind bars and why 500 men and 500 donkeys were taken on to perform the biggest audit in British history.

We'll look too, at some of accountancy's worst nightmares - a rogues' gallery of bankrupts, spendthrifts, fraudsters and embezzlers who, over the years, have made accountants break out into a million cold sweats.

My dear hope is to give you some fun, entertainment and dare I say, perhaps a moment or two of quiet reflection on what you may want and need from your work and your life.

The best-selling British philosopher Alain de Botton believes that work performs two basic purposes - to earn money to survive, and as a distraction from death. Happy thoughts, both! In this book, we'll be looking at just why a career in accountancy can be the most splendid distraction to thoughts about our own mortality....

REASONS TO BE CHEERFUL

Let's begin on a number of truly positive notes. Number one, accountants read more than any other profession in the UK. According to a survey commissioned by World Book Day, people who work in accountancy spend an average of 5.25 hours a week with their noses in a book.

44 per cent of accountants favour contemporary fiction, but their top two favourite books are 'The Lord of the Rings' and Jane Austen's 'Pride and Prejudice'. And just to refute that stereotypical "boring" tag, accountants read more humorous books than any other profession.

Other recent national surveys reveal that accountants take more exotic holidays than most people - and enjoy more active sex lives. 2011's Well Living survey shows that accountants are second only behind doctors in taking part in organised sports and exercise - and perhaps not surprisingly, top in successfully organising their personal financial affairs.

And a 2011 survey from USA News and World Report revealed that during these tough economic times, the most stable and secure profession is accountancy. In the USA alone, they predict a growth in the industry that will see an estimated 60, 000 new jobs appear between 2012 and 2018.

So we're good. Accountancy is officially cool!

TIME FOR A LITTLE HISTORY...

Let me take you back to approximately 3300 BC and the site of the Great Temple in the Sumerian city of Uruk - now part of modern day Iraq. The Sumerians were the first civilisation to practise intensive, year round farming.

With the spread of modern agriculture and irrigation, the prosperity of this ancient world began to grow. More grain was produced and more livestock reared, generating great surpluses of food. Eventually, people's memories could no longer be trusted to keep track of what was being traded and a system needed to be developed to record what was being bought and sold.

In order to keep a close eye on who owed what to whom, early 'accountants' began to issue receipts and IOUs - and accidentally invented writing. Etched onto wedge-shaped clay tablets called cuneiforms, these simple tokens did much to foster the development of civilised societies and the spread of the written word.

The ancient Mesopotamian counting system was based on 60 - hence, the reason we now have 60 seconds in a minute and 60 minutes in an hour.

Accounting in Ancient Egypt was little different from Mesopotamia's rudimentary list-making - though the Egyptians did swap clay tablets for papyrus, which allowed for more detailed records. And in the royal storehouses, audits had to be scrupulously accurate, no matter how huge the task at hand - any mistakes and the accountants were punished with fines, hands and feet being chopped off and even death.

Over in Ancient Greece, things began to move on a little, with the introduction of coinage around 600 B.C.. Early banks began to develop, offering money changing, loans and even cash transfers for citizens travelling to distant cities.

And a few hundred years later, Roman accountants introduced the idea of an annual budget, co-ordinating the empire's diverse financial enterprises. Europe-wide financial planning began to take place, with the empire's expenditure being limited to its estimated yearly revenues. As a result, the Roman taxation system became more organised, rigorous and based more fairly on the ability to pay.

Fast forward to 500 A.D. and Hindu mathematicians in India helped the accounting cause by inventing the 'zero'. But the world over, civilisations were still stuck with simple, laborious list makings. As commerce began to develop around the globe, trading ventures required more capital than one person or company was able to invest - and the need for more detailed methods of accounting became urgent.

In medieval Europe, things were about to change...

LUCA PACIOLI: THE FATHER OF MODERN ACCOUNTANCY?

Dear reader, as I'm sure you know, Luca Pacioli is known as the Father of Accountancy. An Italian monk and mathematician, in 1494 Pacioli wrote what is often referred to as the very first accountancy textbook. In truth, the accountancy element was just part of a larger mathematics tome, snappily entitled 'Summa de arithmetica, geometria, proportioni al proportionality'. But it is meant to include the first complete description of double-entry bookkeeping.

However, there is much proof that a fellow Italian called Amatino Manucci got there before him, nearly 200 years previously. A partner in the Florentine merchant firm of Giovanni Farolfi and Company, Manucci was despatched to the business's French base in the Provence in 1299.

His financial records, which are still in existence, contain the earliest known example of double-entry bookkeeping. Some historical scholars believe that the illustrations which appear in the manuscript were drawn by Pacioli's close friend, a certain Leonardo da Vinci.

So Pacioli or Manucci? Perhaps we'll never know. But one thing's for sure. Pacioli, the wandering monk, had many strings to his bow. He also wrote a series of major works on mathematics, and a seminal treatise about chess.

BIZARRE TAXES

Author, poet and physician Oliver Wendell Holmes once memorably called taxes "the price we pay for civilisation". OK, most of the time we can all accept the necessity of handing over cash to fund essential services and our society's day-to-day needs. But sometimes you get the impression that the gatherers of tax are, well, just taking the mickey!

Throughout history The Taxman has done his or her level best at dreaming up novel new ways of parting us from our hard earned cash. Roman Emperors Nero and Vespasian (AD 69-79) even went so far as to put a tax on urine!

The tax had to be paid by licensed urine collectors who daily emptied the public toilets. At the time, this was a highly lucrative business, as the urine was then sold on to leather workers for use in the tanning process and launderers for whitening togas, thanks to its high ammonia content.

Centuries later, urine became a key component in the production of gunpowder. So there's money in that there urine!

In 1660, Charles II needed an extra £1.2 million a year to shore up the royal coffers, so his men at the treasury hit upon the idea of a Fireplace Tax. Their logic was, the more hearths you had, the richer you must be - and therefore perfectly able to hand over more cash to the king.

Similar logic was used in 1696, when the British Parliament introduced the Window Tax - the more you had, the more you were forced to pay. Look around houses built in the late 17th and early 18th century in London, York, Bristol, Chester and the like, and you'll spot many a bricked up window - done to avoid paying the new tax.

In 1712, Britain even introduced a Wallpaper Tax. Painted, printed or patterned wallpaper was taxed at one old penny per square yard. A deeply unpopular tax (thinking about it, can you name me one that isn't?) it was finally abolished well over 100 years later in 1836.

But perhaps the greatest taxer of them all was Russia's Peter the Great. The mighty ruler's great mission was to modernise his vast nation and to expand its empire. Observing that money was "the artery of war", he set about taxing his people until it hurt.

So keen was he to raise new revenue, the Tsar appointed a full-time royal committee to create ever more bizarre tax laws. Subsequently, taxes were levied on everything from water and beehives, to oak coffins and private bath houses.

Peter the Great also started a tax on beards and moustaches. Passed in 1705, Peter's rationale for this most personal of taxes was that facial hair was archaic and old-fashioned, and he wished for his people to be seen as "clean shaven citizens of modernised Western Europe".

But perhaps the Tsar's strangest tax of all was on something totally invisible. Citizens who didn't believe that human beings had a soul were subject to a religious dissenter's tax.

In 1795, Britain's Prime Minister William Pitt was desperate to raise cash for military forays abroad and in so doing, established the UK's strangest ever tax. At the time, the powdered wig was the epitome of style - so Pitt slapped a tax on wig powder. This caused an absolute outcry amongst the ruling classes, and the levy proved to be short-lived. But this was a tax that changed men's fashion - by 1820 powdered wigs were out of style.

Another century later, in 1895, the United States became yet another government keen to chisel more cash out of its citizens to fund a conflict. In this case, it was the Spanish - American war and to help pay for it, the USA taxed the new-fangled telephone. More specifically, they placed a 3 per cent levy on long distance calls, reasoning that only the wealthy were rich enough to afford telephones.

But as more and more citizens purchased phones, the government realised they'd created a veritable cash cow and kept the tax on the statute book long after the Spanish-American had finished. In fact, over a hundred years more. The long distance telephone tax was finally repealed in 2006.

GRUESOME HISTORICAL TAX FACT!

Being a tax collector can sometimes seriously damage your health. During the French Revolution in 1789, each and every one of the nation's tax collectors were summarily rounded up and then sent to Madam Guillotine.

ONLY IN AMERICA!

Fast forwarding to the modern day, in the staunchly Mormon state of Utah, taxpayers who own businesses where 'nude or partially nude individuals perform any service' are forced to pay a 10 per cent sales and use tax. This applies to all money made from admission fees, plus sales of merchandise, drink and services.

Not that the tax has raised much cash. Staid Utah only has two businesses wild enough to be liable for the levy.

Deep down south in Alabama, if you buy a deck of cards, expect to pay the state's 10 per cent Card Tax. Whilst further north in Maine, it's the blueberry industry who get an extra taxing. Anyone who grows, purchases, sells, handles or processes them is subject to a tax of $0.75 per pound.

Figure this one! If you buy a drink from a soda fountain in Chicago, you'll pay a 9 per cent tax. If you purchase the same soda in a bottle or can, you'll only pay 3 per cent.

And finally, a tax that is not amusing at all - the Amusement Tax. Levied in most states and cities, it's a 10 per cent tax on tickets sold at any entertainment or sporting venue with more than 750 seats.

NOVEL TAX DEDUCTIONS

American stripper Chesty Love (hmmm- I wonder if that's her real name?) had silicone implant surgery to boost the size of her breasts to an eye-watering 56FF, figuring it would help earn her more tips. The IRS initially rejected the claim, but Ms Love took it to court, acting as her own attorney. Finally, the taxmen accepted it as a tax write-off, considering it a stage prop essential to her act.

The US Tax Man also allows pro bodybuilders to claim for body oil to make their muscles glisten, whilst Alaskan whaling captains can claim up to $10,000 for repairing their boats.

But the leading candidate for the strangest of tax deductions? In 1962, the IRS approved a tax write-off that allowed American parents to claim for their children's clarinet lessons. Apparently, the IRS were advised by orthodontists that playing the clarinet helps with kids' overbites.

WEIRD FACT ALERT!

Bookkeeper and other words derived from it - like bookkeeping - are the only words in the English language that have three consecutive double letters.

ONLY AN ACCOUNTANT COULD CATCH AL CAPONE!

The FBI spent years trying to convict brutal mobster Al 'Scarface' Capone through force. But in the end, the gangster was put away thanks to the diligent work of a team of accountants.

During Prohibition, Capone virtually ran the city of Chicago. The son of a law-abiding Italian barber and a seamstress, he owned or controlled hundreds of illegal distilleries, brothels, speakeasies, night clubs and gambling halls. Al personally 'interviewed' all of the prostitutes employed by his clip joints, one of whom gave him syphilis which would ultimately lead to his death. By the late 1920s, his many illegal operations were turning over an estimated $100 million a year - worth billions in present day.

Alphonse Gabriel Capone had the city's politicians, police and law courts in his pocket, and any cases the FBI tried to bring against him collapsed thanks to bribery on a massive scale. Rivals were ruthlessly executed and it is estimated that during his decade long crime career, Capone personally killed or ordered the assassinations of over 500 people.

Most notoriously, it is believed that Capone gave the orders that led to the infamous St Valentine's Day Massacre. Seven members of a rival gang, suspected of hijacking and stealing illegal hooch from Capone, were machine gunned down in cold blood in a garage on North Clark Street, Chicago. Gory press photos of the murdered men lying in pools of their own blood, led to a public outcry, and pressure was put upon the law enforcement agencies to finally nail Capone.

Elliot Ness and his crack FBI 'Untouchables' team tried to force Capone out of business by smashing up and closing down his operations. But as soon as a bar or a brothel was taken out, another would immediately open across the city.

Capone seemed unstoppable - until Forensic Accountant Frank J. Wilson and his team from The Special Intelligence Unit of the Treasury Department became involved in the gangster's activities. It was time to swap the broadsword for the rapier...

Wilson and his men scoured over two million documents seized in raids on Capone's businesses - the aim, to build a tax evasion case against him. Despite being constantly threatened and intimidated by Capone's mobsters, the team spent months forensically scouring coded financial papers and in 1931, they hit pay dirt.

Wilson and his men discovered three ledgers that proved Capone owned a gambling operation that had paid no income tax on its vast profits throughout the 1920s. Capone was charged with tax evasion and the case brought to court. Cocky as ever, Scarface was unconcerned by the charges and got his men to bribe every member of his trial jury.

But at the last minute, aware of his actions, the FBI arranged for the twelve men and women to be switched with a jury from another trial. To his stunned disbelief, Capone was found guilty and sentenced to eleven years in prison, much of it spent in Alcatraz.

Suffering from the advanced stages of syphilis, Capone slowly went mad. He was released from prison in 1939, a shambling shell of a man. He died in Florida in 1947.

As a consequence of their success in putting the mobster away, the IRS actually launched an ad campaign with the boast, "Only An Accountant Could Catch Al Capone".

WEIRD FACT ALERT!

Al Capone's business card described his profession as 'Used Furniture Dealer'. Yeah, right...

THE FAMOUS IN FLAMES

History is littered with celebrities who've fallen foul of the taxman. Sophia Loren famously spent 18 days in an Italian jail for tax evasion, whilst her compatriot, Luciano Pavarotti had to cough up a reported $11 million in unpaid tax in 1999.

Back in 1974, legendary comedian Richard Pryor served 10 days in a Los Angeles county jail for tax evasion. He told the judge at his trial "he just forgot to pay". Bankruptcy also ended the careers of Abbott and Costello, whilst Sammy Davis Jnr owed $7.5 million in unpaid taxes at his death.

Musicians have fared little better when it comes to financial problems. Willie Nelson had to pay $16.7 million in back taxes and suffered the ignominy of having his assets confiscated and auctioned off. Legend has it that sympathetic showbiz chums bought back many of his belongings and simply gave them back to Nelson.

When Grammy-nominated American singer/songwriter Peter Case got into trouble with the tax people, he was soon to learn just how ingenious the IRS can be. A legendary live performer, Case has made much of his money from endless touring. Aware of this, IRS agents would check through music paper gig guides to work out where Case was playing. Once they knew he was on stage, IRS operatives would visit the box office to confiscate his fee and put it towards paying off his back tax.

THE JOE LOUIS STORY

Legendary World Heavyweight boxing champion Joe Louis mashed up 68 opponents during his long professional career, losing just three fights. But his biggest battle was against the Tax Man.

Born in a wood cabin in the cottonfields of Alabama, 'The Brown Bomber' won his first World Heavyweight crown aged just 23 - and then went on to successfully defend it 20 times. Along the way, Louis was hugely generous to family, friends and strangers - but also poorly advised on the financial front. At one point, his managers and trainers were allegedly taking over 75 per cent of his gross earnings.

When America joined the Second World War in 1941, Joe patriotically shelved his lucrative boxing career to become a $21 dollar a month private in the US Army. But not before making two successful final defences of his world crown. He gave his entire earnings of over $100,000 from the fights to the US Army Relief Fund and the Naval Relief Fund. Louis kept not a penny for himself.

At the end of the war, the White House was so overwhelmed by the generosity of Louis's contribution to the war effort on so many different fronts, he was given an official citation thanking him for all his good works. The IRS was not so appreciative.

Throughout the 1940s, America's top marginal rate took an almighty hike to 90 per cent and Joe Louis found himself with a bill for $500,000 in back taxes. The IRS wouldn't even allow The Brown Bomber to deduct the two fight purses he had handed over to the navy and the army. Even more punitively, they refused his claim for $3,000 worth of tickets he'd personally bought to give out free to US servicemen for the bouts.

As interest payments compounded each year, Louis was forced to come out of retirement just to service his tax debt. For the next 20 years, one of sport's greatest heroes fought a losing battle to pay off his debts and died a broken man.

Louis successfully defended his titles 25 times - a record for the heavyweight division. In 2005, he was named the greatest heavyweight of all time by the International Boxing Research Organisation.

Boxing's bible, Ring magazine, ranked Joe Louis number one on their list of the 100 Greatest Punchers of All Time.

SPORTING FACT ALERT!

Accountant Edwin Flack won Australia's first and second gold medals at the inaugural modern Olympics in 1896, triumphing in the 800 and 1500 metres. He also won bronze in the doubles tennis. At the time of the Olympics, he worked in London for Price Waterhouse.

REMBRANDT - AN ACCOUNTANT'S WORST NIGHTMARE

Rembrandt Harmensz van Rijn is generally considered to be one of the most inspirational artists of all time. During his lifetime (1606 - 1669), he was dubbed 'one of the great prophets of civilisation'. His paintings, portraits and sketches are regarded as being amongst the most important works of Dutch art's 'golden age'. Rembrandt was also the man who put the 'F' into feckless.

Picture this. You are the best paid European artist of your age. Every single piece you complete is immediately sold for vast sums of money. Financially, what could possibly go wrong?

Rembrandt lived like a 17th century rock star and became a byword for conspicuous consumption. In 1639, he bought one of the largest and most expensive houses in Amsterdam. Despite his wealth, he struggled to meet the initial payment deadlines. But this didn't stop Rembrandt from spending vast amounts of money on furnishings and art with which to fill the house.

For years, Rembrandt continued to live well beyond his means, and simply painted more canvases when he needed to stave off his debtors. But then a triple disaster struck.

The first Anglo-Dutch war caused a severe economic downturn in Holland, and demand for luxury goods, like art, fell drastically.

Allied to this Rembrandt quite literally became a victim of his own success. His many students increasingly began to offer similar works to Rembrandt's at much cheaper prices.

And it cannot be denied that wealthy art collectors were increasingly staying clear of Rembrandt. His standing as an artist was being constantly eroded by the utter chaos of his personal life. As well as being hopelessly in debt, he was conducting affairs all around Amsterdam, including one with his son's nurse.

Hardly a financial genius, Rembrandt's solution was simply to borrow more money from elsewhere to pay off his debts. Finally, he was forced to declare himself bankrupt.

At the time, German and English debtors faced hellish prisons, earcutting and sometimes execution. Conversely, Holland was staggeringly liberal in its treatment of the feckless. Much more like a modern bankruptcy, the Dutch system allowed Rembrandt the opportunity of a fresh start.

But guess what? Once he was discharged from bankruptcy, Rembrandt again began to live well beyond his means....

HOW THE WIZARD OF OZ WENT BUST

A contender for accountancy's worst nightmare was the Wizard of Oz creator, L. Frank Baum.

'The Wonderful Wizard of Oz' was first published in 1900, and met with instant success. It immediately smashed all extant records for US book sales, and two years later, was adapted into a sell-out stage musical that toured America for years on end. Further Oz novels hit the top of the bestseller lists, earning L. Frank Baum immense celebrity status and a massive fortune.

But Mr Baum was a far better writer than he was a businessman. In 1909, and against all advice, he came up with an idea that would ruin him. He formed his own company to produce hand-coloured slides of scenes from his Oz books. In front of an expensive full orchestra, Baum hired major American theatres for a massive tour, where he would spend the evenings narrating his stories against a backdrop of the slides.

Despite the huge popularity of the Oz books, his ambitious venture was a complete and utter flop. He lost every penny he'd earned and had to file for bankruptcy.

To lift himself out of trouble, Baum set about doing what he did best - furiously churning out idea after idea. In total, he wrote 55 novels (and four "lost novels"); 82 short stories; over 200 poems; and an unknown number of play scripts.

HONEST ABE LINCOLN, INSOLVENT DEBTOR

The sixteenth President of the United States, Abraham Lincoln unified the country after the bitter Civil War; emancipated black slaves, and became one of the most iconic and revered Americans in history.

It's a little known fact that before going into politics, Honest Abe suffered nearly two decades of crippling financial disaster. In 1832, he bought a general store in New Salem, Illinois. A year later, his partner in the venture died, the business was through the floor and Lincoln had to declare it bankrupt.

In the process, he lost his only two remaining assets - a horse and some surveying gear - and spent the next 17 years paying off money he'd borrowed from friends to set up the business and then to try and keep it afloat.

Lincoln was also a trained lawyer, and perhaps not surprisingly, he specialised in debtor-creditor cases.

He was in good - or should that be bad? - company, when it comes to US presidents who were seriously strapped for cash. President Thomas Jefferson filed for bankruptcy several times, whilst William McKinley went bankrupt whilst serving as Governor of Ohio.

THE REAL LIFE SCROOGE

Jolly Bob Cratchit is fiction's most famous clerk's accountant - his boss, Ebenezer Scrooge, the meanest man in fiction. But was he purely the product of Charles Dickens' fertile imagination?

Many historians believe Dickens based Scrooge on a man named John Elwes (formerly John Meggot, but more of that later!). Born in 1714 to a rich Berkshire family, Elwes' life began to unravel when he was four, as his father died. His mother was left a fortune of £100,000, but soon after, died of starvation because she was too mean to spend any of it.

Like mother like son, Elwes immediately picked up the baton of miserliness. He refused to spend money on clothes, and for decades wore threadbare rags. Consequently, he was often mistaken for a beggar and offered money - which he took. He would wear the same clothes in bed, to save on buying nightshirts.

Elwes ate with his servants to save on heating the rest of his house, and often ate rotten food to save on bills. He once complained bitterly about birds robbing him of hay to build their nests.

But his hero and role model was his tightwad uncle, Sir Harvey Elwes, 2nd Baronet of Stoke College and MP for Sudbury. Though fabulously rich, Sir Harvey lived like a pauper and resented spending a penny on, well, anything!

To curry favour with his uncle, in the hope that Sir Harvey might leave him a wad or two, John changed his surname by deed poll from his father's name of Meggot to his uncle's surname, Elwes. And it worked! Sir Harvey died in 1763 and left his nephew a fortune of £250,000 - approximately £18 million in present day dosh.

However, though he was now financially loaded from the proceeds of two separate inheritances, John Elwes allowed his home to fall into total rack and ruin; too mean was he to pay for essential roof repairs and building work. The miser would rather sleep underneath tarpaulins than pay for new tiles on his leaking roof.

Between 1772 and 1784, Elwes served as MP for Berkshire, but he never once rose to address the House. In fact, he seldom attended the House of Parliaments at all, because it would have meant spending money on travel.

Eventually, Elwes became a moneylender and also helped finance the construction of important areas of Georgian London, like Portman Square and parts of Piccadilly and Oxford Circus.

He lived on less than £50 a year for most of his adult life, and when he died, Elwes left an astonishing £500,000 in his will. Based upon per capita GDP, today that would be worth approximately £557,000,000.

THE ACCOUNTANT WHO INVENTED BUBBLE GUM

In 1928, 23-year-old accountant Walter Diemer was employed by the Frank Fleer Chewing Gum company in Philadelphia, USA. He was so enthusiastic about gum, he spent his spare time trying out new recipes.

One day he accidentally knocked up a batch that was less sticky and more flexible than normal gum. He gave it a chew, and then on instinct, tried to blow a bubble with the gum. It worked! Diemer immediately knew he was onto something.

Gum companies, including his own, had spent the previous 20 years unsuccessfully trying to perfect a recipe for gum that would blow bubbles. With his little accident, Diemer had discovered the holy grail of the gum world.

To distinguish it from normal gum, it was decided to make bubble gum a different colour. Apparently, the only food colouring available in the Frank Fleer factory was pink and it's reckoned to be the reason why bubble gum is usually that colour to this very day.

Diemer delivered a five pound lump of his amazing new bubble gum to a local grocery store, where it was cut up into little pieces. Before the day was done, the entire lump had sold out. By the end of 1928, The Frank Fleer company had sold 1.5 million pieces of bubble gum.

Diemer never patented his invention, but happily stayed with the Fleer firm for decades, eventually becoming a senior vice president.

WEIRD FACT ALERT!

Amazing but true, Milton Hershey's first candy store went bankrupt. If at first you don't succeed, try, try again! Which he obviously did with quite some success...

THAT 'BORING ACCOUNTANT' TAG….

As I'm sure you well know much of the 'boring accountant' tag stems from a legendary Monty Python sketch called 'The Lion Tamer'. The inestimable Michael Palin played a 45-year-old accountant called Mr Anchovy who wanted a career move to "something more exciting". John Cleese was the recruitment consultant assigned to advise Anchovy on his new career aspirations.

Aptitude tests were taken and the result…? That Mr Anchovy was ideally suited to be an accountant. Anchovy said he already was: "It's dull. Dull. Dull. My God it's dull. It's so desperately dull and tedious and stuffy and boring and desperately dull".

To which the recruitment consultant chips in with: "Our experts describe you as an appallingly dull fellow, unimaginative, timid, lacking in initiative, spineless, easily dominated, tedious company and having no sense of humour. Whereas in most professions these would be considerable drawbacks, in accountancy they are a positive boon".

But Anchovy will not be deterred. He wants to become a lion tamer! When asked what qualifications he had for the job, Anchovy says that he's seen lions in the zoo and he's bought a Lion Taming Hat. As the sketch collapses into anarchy, Cleese's consultant turns to the camera and duly delivers a public service announcement about the dangers of chartered accountancy.

The Python team loved the sketch so much, they included it in both episode 10 of their first series, and then again, in the film, 'And Now For Something Completely Different'.

There is though, a huge irony to all of this. In the 1980s, John Cleese helped launch what was to become a hugely successful business training video company. Cleese appeared in and produced a goodly number of their films. Including one that extolled the virtues of becoming....yes, you guessed it, an accountant. So ultimately - victory for the profession!

WEIRD FACTOID

What do The Toad Elevating Moment, Vaseline Review and Bun, Owl Stretching Time and Wackett, Buzzard, Stubble and Boot have in common? They were all names considered by Cleese, Palin and crew before they agreed on the moniker, 'Monty Python's Flying Circus'.

ACCOUNTANTS AND COMEDY

So why do accountants so often get it in the neck from comedians? Here's a theory for you - perhaps it's because so many ex-accountants went on to become comedians. No, I'm not joking. They are legion, my friends.

The wonderful Eddie Izzard is one of Britain's comedy greats. Double Emmy award-winning, his rambling, free associating scatological humour ironically owes a great deal to Monty Python's Flying Circus. Famously known to be a transvestite - or as Eddie describes himself, "a male tomboy" - he's fast becoming an accomplished film and TV actor, starring in everything from 'Ocean's Twelve' to the FX drama series, 'The Riches'.

Izzard is also a man of steely single-mindedness. In 2009, despite never having taken part in a long distance run before, he completed a mind-boggling 43 marathons in 51 days, to raise money for charity.

But Eddie wasn't quite so determined in his first choice of career. Izzard enrolled for an Accountancy degree at Sheffield University. He failed his first year exams and though he pleaded to be allowed to do re-sits, Izzard was thrown out. No doubt a disappointment to his dad, Harold Izzard, who worked as Chief Accountant for British Petroleum.

Bob Newhart was a quiet, unassuming guy who worked as an accountant in Chicago. At company parties, he'd struggle to conquer his shyness by doing his 'party trick' - a comedy routine that included a sketch about Abraham Lincoln getting his own publicity agent.

He first worked for a construction materials manufacturer, called United Gypsum, and then briefly, as a clerk for the US Unemployment Office. He quit after discovering that the weekly unemployment benefit was $45 - just ten dollars less than he was earning for a week's work.

Allegedly, his 'motto' at the time was "that's close enough", perhaps suggesting he was never really cut out to be an accountant.

Newhart moved on to work for an advertising copywriter in Chicago, and then dipped his toe into the waters of Middle America's comedy circuit, expecting it to last no more than two years, tops. But his first comedy LP struck a chord with fellow American white collar workers who loved his dry buttoned-down style. The album sold 1.5 million copies - a staggering amount for a then unknown new comedian. The rest is history and over the next 40-plus years, Newhart became a comedy legend.

One of Britain's alternative comedy treasures is Arnold Brown, who bills himself as possibly the only Jewish Glaswegian ex-chartered accountant stand-up comedian in the world. If you don't know anything about Arnold Brown, check him out now. Google him and watch some clips of his act on YouTube. Go watch him live. Buy his laugh out loud comedy novel, 'Are You Looking At Me Jimmy?' Because this guy is a one-off comedy genius.

He's won the Perrier Comedy Award at the Edinburgh Festival; played support to Frank Sinatra in Glasgow's Ibrox Park just before Ol' Blue Eyes died, and has packed out comedy clubs and festivals across the world.

I guess the best way to describe his style is gently surreal, warmly humane and wonderfully scatological. He's a comic philosopher who inspires great affection amongst audiences and almost constant and universal praise from the critics. I love this guy, with good reason.

As your humble author, I must confess to 'previous' with Arnold Brown. Back in the 1990s, I co-wrote two series of his 'Arnold Brown and Company' show on BBC Radio Four. Arnold was a joy to work with - warm, friendly and clubbable, and never precious. He is also one of the most genuinely funny people I've ever had the pleasure to meet. Few people possess 'the funny bone', but Arnold is truly one of them.

Just before I started work on the first series of 'Arnold Brown and Company', I went to watch his stand-up act in Manchester, during a national tour. He duly delivered one of the funniest, ice-breaking opening lines I've ever heard. The venue he was playing, The Green Room, was uber-trendy and alternative, and in truth, sometimes a bit too 'up itself'.

Arnold strode slowly out onto the stage, took the microphone in his hand, smiled at the packed audience and said: 'Hello. Or is that too mainstream for you?' Arnold Brown, we salute you!

Fellow Scots stand up and wit Fred Macaulay also cut his teeth in accountancy. An ever popular regular in TV shows like 'Have I Got News For You?', 'QI' and 'Mock The Week', Fred is an alumni of Dundee University where he read Accountancy and Jurisprudence.

He subsequently became a chartered accountant and then spent three years as company accountant at the family-owned Pitlochry Knitwear Company. By the time he left to make his name on the stand up circuit, it was a PLC with 80 shops and a turnover of £40 million.

Accountancy's loss was comedy's gain - but I bet he still misses getting decent discount on his woolly jumpers.

THAT'S SHOWBIZ!

It's not only comedians who started off their careers in the second oldest profession. A dizzying number of entertainers, musicians, sportsmen and actors have all had their fair share of double entry book-keeping. For example, leather-lunged Led Zeppelin singer Robert Plant left accountancy to try his luck as a singer.

His dad was keen on him becoming an accountant, but Plant only managed two weeks at the ledgers, packed in his job and went to croon in local bands around Birmingham. The rest as they say, is history.

Ever heard of Kenneth Bruce Gorelick? You should have - over the years, he's sold more than 75 million albums.

Better known as jazz sax supremo Kenny G, Kenneth started off playing in Barry White's Love Unlimited Orchestra in 1974, aged just seventeen, and continued to play professionally while majoring in Accounting at the University of Washington in Seattle.

Kenny G's sixth album, 'Breathless', is still the best selling instrumental album of all time, with over 15 million copies sold worldwide.

Best selling author John Grisham received a Bachelor of Science degree in Accounting from Mississippi State University - and then became an accountant's dream.

His books, which include phenomenal best seller 'The Firm', have sold over 250 million copies worldwide. Grisham is one of only three writers to sell two million copies on a first printing - the other two being J.K. Rowling and Tom Clancy.

Actor Ron Moody, who famously played Fagin in the movie 'Oliver', took an Accountancy degree at the London School of Economics.

Golfer Padraig Harrington gained an Accountancy degree from the Dublin Business College, and credits his accountant's training with giving him the discipline to organise and manage his life as a golfer.

Already a top amateur golfer as a student, the ever-pragmatic Paidraig decided to study accountancy in case he didn't make it as a pro, so that he would have the "tools" to work in the game as a player's personal manager or running a golf course.

Lee Van Cleef was one of cinema's greatest ever villains, perhaps best known for his bad guy roles in a spaghetti westerns like 'For A Few Dollars More' and 'The Good, The Bad and The Ugly'. But it's a little known fact that Van Cleef started off his working life as a trainee accountant.

Born Clarence LeRoy Van Cleef Jnr in New Jersey, he left school and got a job as a junior in a local accountancy firm. In the evenings, he trod the boards with an amateur dramatics society, which led to an offer from a professional touring theatre company. It was whilst he was out on the road, acting in a long forgotten play called 'Mr Roberts', that he got a lucky break.

In the audience one night was movie director Stanley Kramer, who liked what he saw. Van Cleef was duly cast as Jack Colby in 'High Noon'.

In all of the research I did for this book on former accountant celebrities, one discovery shocked me more than any other. That one of rock music's most notorious bad boys Gibby Haynes trained as an accountant.

For over 20 years, Haynes was lead vocalist in one of the toughest, most uncompromising US bands around, The Butthole Surfers. Variously described as hardcore, punk and industrial metal, the group were just plain noisy, snotty and famous for their extreme drug taking lifestyles.

What the band's biog didn't contain? The fact that Haynes was not only an Accountancy major at Texas's Trinity University, but memorably, a one-time Accounting Student of the Year.

A man of many parts, Gibby was also the star captain of the Trinity University basketball team and is now a talented artist who regularly exhibits in New York's hippest galleries.

And if you think The Butthole Surfers goes to the extreme as a band moniker, have a squint at earlier names they flirted with - Fred Astaire's Asshole, and The Ashtray Babyheads.

More recently, Haynes has been playing and recording with his best mate Johnny Depp in the band P.

WEIRD GIBBY HAYNES FACT!

His dad is actor Jerry Haynes, best known as the host of popular US childrens' TV show, Mr Peppermint.

TEN THINGS I'VE LEARNT ABOUT BEING AN ACCOUNTANT

"Ten Facts I've Learnt About..." is a regular feature on the hugely successful 'David Letterman Show' in the USA. Letterman invited ten accountants - eight men and two women - onto the show to pass on their wisdom. In no particular order, here are the ten things they claim to have learnt about their profession...

1. When you know the right people at the Post Office, it can be April 15th whenever you want. (NB: April 15th is US tax pay-up day!)
2. People will pay you a lot of money if you pretend you know how the tax code works.
3. Wite-Out and 7-Up is strangely refreshing. (NB: Wite-Out is the US version of Tipp-Ex)
4. If you're confused by something on your tax form, just write "huh"?
5. You do the taxes: don't let the taxes do you.
6. The only thing more satisfying than getting a client a sizeable refund, is the garlic shrimp scampi at Red Lobster. (NB: Red Lobster is a very popular New York restaurant).
7. Numbers is hard.
8. After completing tax returns for 12 straight hours, your calculator starts talking to you.
9. Always put your clients first - unless you get an offer to go on Letterman.
10. And my favourite, delivered by balding, bespectacled accountant Richard Cohen.... "Women want me. Men want to be me".

THE BIGGEST MONEY SCAM OF ALL TIME ?

It was called Operation Bernhardt. During World War Two, Hitler's money men launched an audacious plan aimed at completely destabilising the British economy. The idea? To flood Britain with millions of pounds of worthless notes that would drive the nation towards bankruptcy.

But the supreme irony was that Nazi Germany's currency-making experts just weren't up to the job. The counterfeit notes they produced were too poor in quality and clearly distinguishable from the real thing. Their need for help was so great that the Nazis were forced to turn to a group of men that they cruelly despised - 142 Jewish printers and currency experts whom the fascist regime had imprisoned in Germany's concentration camps.

They were placed together in a 'gilded cage' in Sachsenhausen KZ camp, away from the hellish conditions experienced by the other Jewish inmates. The men were given clean clothes, proper food and regular showers and, as long as they continued to produce high quality work, were treated comparatively well by the camp guards assigned to them.

Faced with the choice between death or collaboration, the inmates developed and produced counterfeit notes that are to this day, regarded as the most perfect ever issued, complete with utterly authentic looking watermarks and serial numbers. Just to give you some idea of how good these counterfeit notes were, in 1960, fifteen years after the end of World War Two, Operation Bernhardt counterfeit notes were still circulating throughout the British banking system.

The Nazi plan was to drop tens of millions of pounds worth of the counterfeit notes over Britain, via the Luftwaffe.

Though over 134 millions worth were printed, in the end, the Luftwaffe were too pressed on the Eastern and Western fronts to free planes to make the surprise delivery. Some notes found their way into the British Isles, but it was in the thousands not the millions.

Operation Bernhard inspired the superb 2007 film, 'Die Falscher', ('The Counterfeiters'), which became the first Austrian movie to win an Oscar - for Best Foreign Language film. And talking of movies…

TEN MOVIES THAT FEATURE ACCOUNTANTS!

THE APARTMENT.

Jack Lemmon starred as put-upon accountant C.C Baxter, who let his boss use his apartment for an illicit affair with Shirley MacLaine. But in the end, C.C. Baxter got the gal!

SHALLOW GRAVE.

Former Doctor Who Christopher Eccleston got good and gory in this Brit horror flick, playing chartered accountant David Stephens.

DAVE.

Another accounting star! Charles Grodin plays the US President's accountant who, overnight, solves the nation's budget deficit. Like you do...

MIDNIGHT RUN.

Charles Grodin loves being an accountant! He returned to the profession in this rollercoaster of a movie, playing a bookkeeper on the run, after embezzling $15 million from a Las Vegas gangster. This brilliant action comedy also stars Robert de Niro.

THE PRODUCERS.

Gene Wilder plays mild-mannered accountant Leo Bloom to Zero Mostel's theatre impresario Max Bialystock. Together, the madcap duo sell 25,000 per cent of the stake in a terrible new play they are confident will flop, to a string of little old ladies. Contains one of the most outrageous musical numbers ever - the sublime 'Springtime For Hitler'.

SCHINDLER'S LIST.

Ben Kingsley plays accountant Itzhak Stern in this gripping war-time drama. Schindler is a German industrialist with a conscience, who sets up a factory using exclusively Jewish labourers, to save them from being sent to the concentration camps. Stern is the Jewish accountant who makes it all happen.

MOONSTRUCK.

The uber-glamorous Cher plays the lead, Loretta Castorini - an Italian American who works as an accountant for small local businesses in Brooklyn. Rated as one of the best romantic comedies of all time, Moonstruck, released in 1987, grossed over $80 million at the American box office. Cher won the Best Actress Oscar for her performance. Bet her accountant was pleased...

LOOK WHO'S TALKING?

Kirstie Alley plays Mollie - a single mum accountant who's looking for a reliable boyfriend. Also starring John Travolta and the voice of Bruce Willis. Erm, that's it...

SHAWSHANK REDEMPTION.

Yes, there was an accountant in this acclaimed prison drama. As the film opened, Andy Dufresne (played brilliantly by Tim Robbins) is a bank worker. Accused of murdering his wife and her lover, he is banged away for life. During his time behind bars, he becomes the jail's unofficial accountant and bookkeeper.

And finally, best movie about accountants ever....

CHRISTIE MALRY'S OWN DOUBLE ENTRY.

The only film in cinema history to fully explain the double entry book keeping system! It's also a pitch black comedy, featuring Nick Moran as Christie Malry - a sinister book-keeper who creates his own "accounting system", committing deadly crimes to balance out slights he believes have been made against him by society.

Malry sets out to balance the books with society by starting small - scrawling graffiti and causing minor public disturbances. By the end of the movie, he's moved onto major urban terrorism.

Directed by Paul Tickell, this neglected 2000 British movie had to wait years for its release, because of a lack of a willing distributor. And perhaps not surprisingly. In the wake of 9/11, distributors stayed well clear of a film whose main character planted bombs underneath Westminster and poisoned London's water supply.

It's a surreal trip of a film that includes flashbacks to 15th century Italy, where Luca Pacioli shows us how he invented the double entry book keeping system.

Uncut magazine named it their Best Film of 2000. And for indie music fans, the haunting soundtrack was written by singer and frontman of The Auteurs, Luke Haines.

THE SHIRT OFF HIS BACK

Between 1997 and 2004 Sir Nicholas Montagu led the Inland Revenue through some of the biggest changes in its 200 year history.

A popular and well-liked civil servant, he achieved an accolade never before given to a senior member of the Inland Revenue - to wit, being voted Personality of the Year by the readers of Accountancy Age.

But as boss of the Inland Revenue, it won't surprise you that Sir Nicholas was not popular with everyone. A much in demand speaker on the after-dinner speaking circuit, he revels in re-telling the story of how one aggrieved tax payer set about letting him know just what he thought of his stewardship.

The man had been stung with a large claim for back tax and feeling that the Inland Revenue had effectively ripped the shirt off his back, decided that Sir Nicholas should experience the same. Driven by a mix of wit and a desire for retribution, the man paid for Sir Nick to become a member of a nudist colony.

Another annoyed tax payer sent Mr Montagu a letter which pointedly observed that "Sir Nicholas Montagu, Chairman of the Inland Revenue", is an anagram of "he'll receive a mountain of cash, nothing remains".

THE GREAT STORK DERBY

Do you have any eccentric millionaires on your books? If so, they'd have to be pretty off the wall to match Canadian Charles Vance Millar. During his lifetime, the millionaire was famous for his practical jokes - most aimed at puncturing hypocrisy. But it was with his will that Millar achieved lasting renown as a big-time eccentric.

When he died in 1925 with no close relatives, he decided to leave a number of playful bequests in his will. These included $700,000 worth of shares in the O'Keefe Brewery, which he left to seven Toronto Methodist ministers who were prominent in the temperance movement. He left his holiday home in Jamaica to three local businessmen who were known to openly loathe and detest one another, on the proviso that they took joint vacations there together.

But Millar's coup de grace was a clause in his will that required the balance of his estate to be converted into money ten years after his death, and the whole amount given to whichever Ontario woman had given birth to the most children during that time. The 'contest' became known as 'The Great Stork Derby'.

The Supreme Court of Canada and a number of Millar's distant relatives fought to invalidate the will. But to no avail. In 1936, four women, who produced nine children each during that time, shared a $750,000 fortune.

THE PATRON SAINT OF ACCOUNTANCY

St Matthew is the patron saint of accountants, book keepers, bankers and tax collectors - and perhaps rather more bizarrely, security guards. Before becoming a disciple, he worked as a tax collector for the Romans in Capernaum, a settlement on the shores of the Sea of Galilee.

In the first century A.D., tax collectors were (surprise, surprise!) reviled by the populace, being regarded as utterly corrupt, readily bribeable and generally 'unclean'. Jesus was heavily criticised for first fraternising with Matthew, but answered his critics by saying: "I came not to call the righteous but the sinners".

Matthew is believed to be one of the few who witnessed both the Resurrection and The Ascension, and wrote the first gospel of the New Testament. Little else is known about the detail of his life, but we know more about his gruesome death. The poor chap had an axe sunk into his head in Egypt by anti-Christians.

If you want to celebrate your patron saint, Matthew's feast day is September 21.

STRANGE FACT ALERT

Though Saint Isidore of Seville lived around 600 A.D., he is the Patron Saint of Computers.

DAMMIT, ACCOUNTANCY IS ROCK'N'ROLL!

Music is so potent. The soundtrack to our lives. It's important that music reflects all of our experiences in the crazy world of the 21st century, and accountancy is currently well-served by two great acts....

Step forward Steve Zelin - by day, an Internal Auditor at a French investment bank in New York; by night, a singer-songwriter who writes tunes about taxes, taking sick days and dealing with the IRS. His CDs include 2008's 'No Accounting For The Holidays', as well as songs with industry-relevant titles like 'I Love To Count', 'IRS Jingle Bells' and 'Stealing From The Company'.

The 'Singing CPA' has a big following amongst accountants in the USA and is often booked for big corporate accountancy events and conferences.

A few hundred miles West in Louisville, Kentucky, four piece band 'The Accountants' is made up entirely of trained accountants, who are also men on a mission.

Here's their manifesto - and it's worth quoting in full....

"We're not really on the warpath, but The Accountants are on a mission of sorts. We wrote these songs for you, the people of America that get up every day and go to work. Whether you drive your own car, take the train, fly or walk to work, there's a certain amount of crap we have to put up with even before we get to work. And then the games begin - the things people do that take the enjoyment out of the jobs most of us liked doing at one time.

Somebody has to do something. We want to raise our voices through music about what it means to live and work in Corporate America. And depending on where you're standing, some of it is pretty damned funny. And some of it is pretty damned sad, too. Some of it will make the perpetrators downright mad or at least, we hope so. And for those who don't like it, please be assured, we won't be laughing with you, we'll be laughing at you.

Now understand, we are not rebels. But we do have a message we wish to impart. And that message stems from our work as part of Corporate America working alongside every one of you. We know what it means to hire, fire, mire and retire and just about everything in between. There's a lot we love about Corporate America and a lot we could do without. We love the fact that there are a few enlightened companies and CEOs who know how to treat their employees, customers and stakeholders.

But there are far too many companies and CEOs who completely miss the point. Their attitude is strictly grab what I can while I can and the wake that's left behind me will be someone else's problem when I'm gone. Unfortunately, this seems to have become the rule rather than the exception. And who is ultimately left holding the bag of shit when they've killed the goose that laid the golden egg? Who else, you and me. Whatever happened to stewardship - leaving it a little better than you found it?

Most of us have to accept what some manager or executive in their infinite wisdom decides to give to us. And the reality is that most boards of directors and executive managers are going to do what they want to do whether you and I like it or not. But that shouldn't stop us from speaking out about what we don't like. Or should it? Oh yeah, I guess they always have that diabolical lever they can pull to have us fired. That's fine. Let The Accountants be your spokespersons. We are all too happy to to write a song to tell the world your story.

Let's take the topic of executive compensation for example. ...let us start by saying we will never criticise anyone who makes a lot of money; after all, this is America and capitalism rules. But for God's sakes, does anyone really need to make fifty or a hundred or several hundred million dollars for running a successful company? Especially when that success, while often very subjective and questionable, comes at the expense of employees who toiled for years to get that CEO where they are.

We're talking about the phenomenon of the mass lay-offs, downsizings and rightsizings. These are people's lives; these are people who have families...people who worked hard for you, Mr CEO. And now you show utter indifference to them by offering them an early out package that makes you feel good about letting them go....how many jobs could have been saved if you took a little less? How many people would you have around you to help the organisation get stronger and smarter and more efficient and help you manage through the tough times that are surely ahead? On will you just foist the same work on fewer people and pay yourself another million dollar bonus or stock grant because you're so smart? Well folks, we've got news for you. It doesn't take brains to do what you've done, just pure unadulterated greed.

The other thing we despise about how much you pay yourselves is that there are no adverse consequences for you if you fail. And this is the part where you've lied to everyone. It's about risk. You've told everyone that you're such a great manager and you put part of your compensation at risk....it's your employees who take all the risk. You want to understand risk?

Try explaining yourself to a single mother of two who just lost her job in one of your so-called restructuring manoeuvres. You should try a new concept - it's called leadership. The employees don't work for you: you should work for them! Give them everything they need to succeed in carrying out the mission and you'll succeed too. Set direction and steer the ship - that's great! But when the ship starts taking on water, you don't start throwing your employees overboard. Take one for the team for a change, instead of showing everyone that you never really cared about anyone but yourself."

Does any of this ring bells? I thought that that was worth sharing in its entirety, because these guys are championing what's fair, decent and honest, so get onto their My Space site and give them a listen.

THE 0.5 PER CENT CAMPAIGN STARTS HERE!

The Accountants are a rocking band, and they shine a spotlight on some very important issues. I would argue that their clearly heartfelt concerns should lead us into a discussion about a seldom talked about problem amongst accountants. It's called stress.

Many of you experience it. Sometimes it can push people to the extremes. Sometimes it can shove them into a dark, dark void where every working day becomes yet another playing out of pain and anguish.

Let's look at some hard facts. At any given time, a quarter of British accountants are off work as a result of stress-related illnesses. Suicide rates amongst male accountants are 10 per cent above the UK national average. More frighteningly, female accountants have three times the UK national average suicide rate for women. It is estimated that one third of accountants in Britain drink to excess, and many of those go on to develop more serious medical and work problems as a result.

Apart from some wonderful and enlightened examples, accountancy firms around the globe seem to be in complete denial about these statistics. In my opinion, they have to get real, get human and pro-active, and offer you much more help, support and understanding. You cannot demand that employees give their all for the firm and then deny all responsibility for their well being, when stress pushes them into worrying and dangerous areas.

It is time for accountancy companies - large and small - to truly acknowledge the pressure that many of their workers feel and put money, thought and energy into helping pull them through the tough times.

And thus, I propose a brand new campaign! Talk to your bosses. Buttonhole your human resources people. Mobilise your co-workers. And get them to agree to the 0.5 per cent rule. To wit, 0.5 per cent of your company's annual profit is paid into an Employees' Welfare Fund, which would pay for counselling, psychological, psychiatric and medical help and practical support with addictions.

Until firms start to come out of denial and address the hard facts of work stress and how that can impact upon their often hugely pressured employees, really good workers will continue to fall by the wayside and rob the industry of skilled and talented people. Please, bosses - wise up. I'm only talking 0.5 per cent of your profits. The benefits could be huge. And you could sleep at night, knowing you've made a truly positive step forward in helping fellow human beings overcome problems and difficulties in their lives. It's got to make good sense all the way round.

WHAT'S IN A NAME?

Manchester Chartered Accountant Thomas Sharples lived extremely frugally on just sixpence a day and by the time of his death, had managed to amass a fortune of £78,000. Did he leave it to his family? Sort of...

The entire amount was to be divided up between anyone over the age of sixty who earnt less than £40 a year - and was called Sharples or Hesmondhalgh.

THE LASERMONKS!

As unlikely stories go, this one takes the whole box of biscuits - a tale from the turn of the 21st century that involves a group of monks and a multi-million dollar ink cartridge business.

Father Bernard McCoy was Steward of Temporal Affairs at the Cistercian Abbey, Our Lady of Spring Bank, Wisconsin, USA. Needing some ink for the abbey's printer, Father McCoy was shocked at the cost of cartridges. After a little research, he found that some companies were making 1,000-2,000 per cent profit on the items.

An idea struck him. If the abbey could negotiate deals with manufacturers, they could cut out the middle man and save schools, churches, public organisations and charities a fortune - and generate a much-needed modest income for the abbey. Lasermonks.com was born.

The venture started slowly, but with the free help of two social entrepreneurs, Sarah Caniglia and Cindy Griffith, Lasermonks developed a reputation for "commerce with compassion". Profits are used to fund charitable works and the company is now used as a best practice business model for would-be social entrepreneurs.

In 2002, the project contained a few monks dealing with a couple of orders a day, with a first year turnover of just $2,500. The company now generates millions of dollars a year.

LUCKY BREAK

On November 25th, 1999, Seattle businessman Ken Ahroni was celebrating both Thanksgiving and his 47th birthday with family, when the diners began to squabble about who should get to pull the turkey wishbone.

A thought occurred to him - why, at Thanksgiving, when families are enjoying a veritable bounty of food, is there but one lonely wishbone to pull? Ahroni had what seemed like a crazy idea. Why not manufacture plastic wishbones for those who felt they needed a lucky break at Thanksgiving?

Through trial and error, he developed a form of brittle plastic that would ensure his wishbones would look - and break - just like the real thing. Marketing the bones as great stocking fillers and impulse buys, his new product captured the public's imagination. Since set up, Ahroni's wishbones have sold in their millions.

The company's packaging carries a disclaimer: "Lucky Break Wishbone Corp. makes no guarantee that our product will make your wishes come true", it reads, "but they might!"

TAXING TIMES IN ATHENS

Greece has for some time had a bit of a reputation for tax evasion. But since its recent financial problems, the Government has been trying to crack down hard on the nation's tax dodgers.

In 2011, after repealing a national privacy law, the Greek finance department issued a public "Name and Shame' list of the worst offenders. Over four thousand individuals appeared on the roster of naughtiness, owing approximately 15 billion euros between them.

Topping the list, and owing an eye-watering 952 million euros in arrears, was a convicted tax fraud, who is already behind bars on a 504 year sentence for handing out fake receipts to firms that wanted to lower their tax bills. Beware Greeks bearing gifts!

Other notables on the roster included the husband of a former government minister, a former pro basketball player and a prominent Greek singer.

DON'T MESS WITH THE IRS!

The mighty US tax department are ever alert to Americans trying to shave what they owe on their tax by... ahem... pushing the envelope somewhat. Here's my favourite from recent years...

In 2008, a Pittsburgh furniture store owner in financial difficulties, hired an arsonist to torch his business. The man's insurance company investigated the fire, and eventually stumped up $500,000 to the ex-store owner.

All would have gone swimmingly well if the businessman hadn't then done something very stupid. The owner dutifully reported the pay out on his income tax return. But along with stating the proper deductions for the building, its contents and the usual business expenses, the moron also deducted a $10,000 'consultation fee' he'd paid his arsonist.

Two years later, the IRS conducted an audit on his accounts - the businessman and his arsonist friend both ended up in prison.

ACCOUNTANTS FROM HELL – JAMES BROWN

No, not THAT James Brown! This James Brown is decidedly unfunky. Though best known in the accountancy world as the very first President of the Institute of Accountants, Brown was a key figure in the eviction of hundreds of peasant farmers in the mid 19th century Highland Clearances in Scotland.

It was the time of an economic downturn and many Highland landlords had gone bankrupt. Their insolvent estates were placed in the hands of men like James Brown, to maximise revenue to pay off creditors. Brown's approach to the situation involved throwing uneconomic tenant families off their land, to make way for far more profitable sheep farmers and deer forests.

What this meant in practice was that already dirt poor subsistence farmers were deprived of their livings and their homes, forced to live rough on scrubland next to the coast or pressured into being shipped across the Atlantic, to be used as virtual slave labour on farms and estates in Canada and the USA. Many died in the process.

Amazingly, Brown himself didn't remotely consider his actions to be cruel or inhumane. On the contrary, he saw himself as a man on a moral mission. He described his evictees as being "reared in poverty and ignorance...many had never been within the walls of a church." Brown claimed to have been motivated by "feelings of humanity, pity and benevolence", sure that the now starving, homeless tenant families would be much better off if they emigrated - whether they liked it or not.

WALTER GENEWEIN - THE ACCOUNTANT OF DEATH

In 1987, a customer rooting around in a secondhand bookshop in Vienna, discovered a strange collection of 400 colour slides. On further investigation, they turned out to be a series of images shot between 1939 and 1944 in Poland's Lodz Ghetto. Each of the pictures was taken by the Nazi's Chief Accountant, Walter Genewein.

Having confiscated a top of the range camera from a Jewish slave labourer, he cheerfully set about recording the inhabitants of Lodz ghetto to showcase "sub-humans in the process of being civilised by the German culture of work and organisation".

The photos were used by Polish film maker, Dariusz Jablonski, as the basis for his critically-acclaimed documentary, 'The Photographer', which told the sinister story of Genewein - and why a ghetto in Poland needed an accountant.

In 1940, the Nazis forced 200,000 Jews into a sealed, self-governing ghetto on the outskirts of Lodz. Conditions were horrific, food was scarce - disease and starvation was rife. The inhabitants were forced to make munitions, uniforms, boots and equipment for the SS. As Chief Accountant, Genewein managed the ghetto's "efficiency of production".

At the time, he commented: "To us, a working Jew is capital to be used, like a machine in a large, well organised company."

Overworked and underfed, many thousands died in wretched squalor. But even in death, Genewein managed to turn a profit on the unfortunates in Lodz ghetto.

Hair was cut from the dead and sent to felt-making factories. The resultant profits all carefully accounted for by Genewein. Body parts were sold on for medical research; gold teeth extracted and wedding rings cut from fingers.

Genewein managed to feather his own nest, too. He stole money, jewellery and valuables confiscated from Lodz's Jewish inhabitants - some of which he gave as presents to his wife.

JOHN LIST - CHARTERED ACCOUNTANT AND MASS MURDERER

One of America's most notorious murderers, List worked for a New Jersey accountancy firm. In November, 1971, he was fired by his company. Already $11,000 in arrears on his mortgage and in wider financial troubles, List drove back to his Westfield home and shot his wife Helen and mother Alma dead. List waited until his daughter Patricia and son Frederick returned home from school and then killed them, too.

He got into his car and went to watch his eldest son John Jnr play in a soccer game. List drove John Jnr home, made him a sandwich and then shot him dead.

The killer accountant had planned his death spree meticulously. Papers and milk had been cancelled and he'd told neighbours and his children's schools that the family were going away on a holiday for a few weeks. It was a month later, before anyone realised that List had butchered his entire family. By this time, he had made good his escape and assumed a new identity hundreds of miles away.

As a decoy, he had parked up his Chevy Impala at Kennedy Airport. The police checked out hundreds of leads, but to no avail.

List evaded capture for a further 18 years, living under the name Robert Peter Clark. He lived in Denver, Colorado, and then Midlothian, Virginia, remarried and resumed work as an accountant.

But in 1989, List was finally flushed out, thanks to the TV programme 'America's Most Wanted'. New Jersey Police had approached the show in a final bid to track List down.

A forensic artist made a clay bust to show what an older List would look like. It was remarkably accurate, and one of "Robert Peter Clark's" neighbours tipped off the police.

List was arrested, given five life sentences and died in Trenton Prison, aged 82, in 2008. Chillingly, he never expressed remorse and claimed he had never considered suicide because he believed that would have barred him from heaven, where he was hoping to be reunited with his family.

HOW TO PAY NO TAX AT ALL

In 1969 - the very year that Irish writer Samuel Beckett won the Nobel Prize for Literature – Ireland's government decided that writers, musicians, artists, sculptors and composers should all be exempt from paying tax.

The law, guided through the Irish parliament by future Prime Minister Charles Haughey, decreed that income from all works of art - from novels, songs and paintings to plays and sculpture - should not be taxed.

Bestselling British author Frederick Forsyth - of 'Day of the Jackal' fame - moved to Ireland after the law was passed, to which Charles Haughey observed: "The plan was not so much to bring you bastards in, but to stop the outflow of Irish talent".

Footnote: Before becoming a politician, Charles Haughey worked as an accountant.

YOU CAN'T TAKE IT WITH YOU!

Let me take you back to Victorian England and the first golden age of capitalism. Britain and its Commonwealth was awash with dosh for its movers and shakers.

Charles Darwin made a few bob from his books, lectures and personal appearances, and when he died in 1882, left an estate worth £146,911 - in today's terms, that's roughly £13 million.

The King of Chocolate, committed Quaker John Cadbury, died with £43,773 in the bank - worth around £4.2 million today. The best of the century's writers made hitherto unknown fortunes from the written word. When Charles Dickens died in 1870, he left £80,000 - £7.1 million in today's terms. Sherlock Holmes creator of Arthur Conan Doyle left the equivalent of £3 million.

But perhaps not surprisingly, the political writer Karl Marx who coined the phrase "all property is theft" and authored the Communist Manifesto, died as he lived - hard-up.

When Marx popped his clogs in 1883, he left an estate worth just £250 - £23,000 in today's money - to his youngest daughter, Eleanor. Though born into a wealthy family in Tier, Germany, Marx lived much of his adult life on hand-outs - most of them coming from his rich friend, successful industrialist, Friedrich Engels.

FANTASTIC FINANCIAL QUOTES

"The avoidance of taxes is the only intellectual pursuit that carries any reward" - John Maynard Keynes

"My problem lies in reconciling my gross habits with my net income" - Errol Flynn

"What good is money if it can't inspire terror in your fellow man?" – Mr Burns, 'The Simpsons'.

"People who complain about paying too much tax can be divided into two types - men and women" – Anon.

"Getting money is not all a man's business: to cultivate kindness is a valuable part of the business of life" - Samuel Johnson

"Accountants are the witch doctors of the modern world and willing to turn their hand to any type of magic" - British judge Charles Eustace Harman

"Money is better than poverty, if only for financial reasons" - Woody Allen

"I have no use for bodyguards, but I have very specific use for two highly-trained, certified public accountants" - Elvis Presley

"The hardest thing in the world to understand is income tax" - Albert Einstein

"The haggis and European Tax Law have much in common. They both involve bloody processes, the end results are a mystery and those of a squeamish disposition should not get involved in the making of either" – Anon.

"Of course I'm doing something about my overdraft: I'm seeing my accountant" - British cartoonist and writer Barry Fantoni

"The pen is mightier than the sword, but no match for the accountant" - British journalist Jonathan Glancey

"The company accountant is shy and retiring. He's shy a quarter of a million dollars. That's why he's retiring" - Milton Berle

"Where large sums of money are concerned, it is advisable to trust nobody" - Agatha Christie in 'The Queen of Crime'

THE WEIMAR REPUBLIC - AN ACCOUNTANT'S NIGHTMARE !

In the early 1920s, Germany was brought to its knees by political violence, strikes and the crippling debt of the reparations that they were forced to pay to the Allied nations in compensation for World War One.

To counter its problems, the beleaguered German government printed vast amounts of new currency. No prizes for guessing what happened...

It caused the second worst bout of hyperinflation that the Western World has ever seen (* more on the worst, later!). At the outbreak of WW1, the Mark was worth 4.2 US Dollars. By August 1923, this had risen to one million per US Dollar. Just four short months later in December 1923, the US Dollar was worth a staggering four trillion German marks.

Three hundred paper mills and 150 printing companies worked around the clock to print the new currency. Buried beneath a mountain of worthless banknotes, the population was driven to the very limits of its endurance. To keep up with the spiralling inflation, workers had to be paid three times a day. And after each payment, family members would rush to the shops to buy up what food they could. Eventually, people needed a sack of notes to pay for a loaf of bread.

Life in Germany became something akin to sitting in the back of a taxi watching the clock click round. In Berlin and Munich restaurants, meals would cost appreciably more when the bills actually arrived at the table than when they were ordered. In some cases, up to 50 per cent more!

In the towns and cities, the shops gradually began to run out of food. Farmers became unwilling to hand over their produce for what was basically worthless money and soon food riots broke out. Farms and shops were robbed and looted and by the end of 1923, Germany faced total economic collapse.

Oh what a joy it must have been to be an accountant in Weimar Germany. During the most depressed and depressing period of modern Germany's economic history, an accountant's biggest fear was that few, if any, of their clients would ever manage to stump up their accountancy fees.

Businesses increasingly withheld their taxes and refused to submit accounts, afraid that the turbo-inflation would leave them paying utterly disproportionate amounts of tax. Hundreds of accountancy firms went to the wall. Those that stayed in business were reduced to paying their employees in potatoes and second hand clothes.

By December 1923, only one per cent of government income was derived from taxes - the other 99 per cent came from the creation of new currency. The country was on its knees.

But in 1924, the nation was saved from bankruptcy by draconian new money and tax reforms. In desperation, the government created a new currency, the Rentenmark, whose issue was strictly limited, and they imposed drastic and swingeing new taxes.

Though saved from total economic collapse, life for the average German continued to be a grinding struggle - thousands were bankrupted; millions were robbed of their livelihoods, and German industry was decimated. Sadly as we now know, this created a fertile soil in which the vile and inhuman roots of Nazism began to grow.

If you want to find out more about this amazing passage of financial and social history, I would highly recommend a remarkable book written by British historian Adam Fergusson, entitled, 'When Money Dies: The Nightmare of the Weimar Collapse'.

Bad though life must have been in Weimar Germany, imagine yourself in Hungary in 1945-46. This is where the Western World's most horrific spell of hyperinflation occurred. Between August 1945 and July 1946 the general level of prices in Hungary rose at the utterly humongous rate of 19,000 per cent per month.

It also resulted in the creation of the world's highest denomination banknote, the one milliard Pengo. Issued in 1946, it was expressed in numbers as 1,000,000,000,000,000,000,000. At the time, it was worth about 20 cents.

MORE FUNNY MONEY...

During the Second World War, metal for armaments was in short supply. So many countries resorted to the production of small denomination banknotes as a temporary substitute for coins. As a consequence, in 1944, Morocco issued the smallest ever banknote - the 50 centimes note. Measuring just 43mm x 31mm, it was the size of a small postage stamp.

And the largest ever banknote? You'd need a very big wallet to hold the mighty Philippines 100,000 peso note. Issued in 1998 to mark the nation's 100 years of independence from Spain, the note actually cost 180,000 pesos to buy! Just one thousand of the notes were printed, aimed squarely at the banknote collectors market.

Printed in Germany, the 100,000 peso note measured a whopping 355.6mm x 215.9mm. In other words, bigger than a sheet of A4 paper.

And talking of pesos, spare a thought for the red-faced coinmakers of Chile. In 2008, they issued 50 million peso coins onto the market that contained the words, 'Republica de Chiie'.

'SO YOU WANT TO BE AN ACCOUNTANT..."

You know the score: you have an interview for a new job, so you do your homework. Research the company, its wants, needs and areas of interest and excellence. You rehearse answers to likely questions and get yourself as fully prepared as possible. And then the interviewing panel throw you a question that seems to defy logic.

Here are just a few genuine curve balls tossed to interviewees looking for jobs in accountancy and the financial services in the US and the UK...

- How many hair salons are there in Japan?
- Why are manhole covers round?
- What is the probability of throwing 11 and over with two dice?
- How do you measure nine minutes using only a four minute and seven second hourglass?
- What should it cost to rent Central Park for commercial purposes?
- Are your parents disappointed with your career aspirations?
- What made you move to a backward city like this?
- What would I find in your refrigerator?
- Which is prettier - a daffodil or a one pound coin?

YOU MUST BE JOKING!

* Why did the auditor cross the road? Because he looked in the file and that's what they did last year.

* A firm were looking to employ a new accountant, and their interviewing panel decided to throw a curve ball to their first interviewee. As the woman sat down and settled herself, the head of the panel asked: 'So tell me, what is two plus two?'

The interviewee put a finger to her lips and went to the door of the office to check that no-one was listening in. She crept over towards the window, drew the blinds and then quietly checked the office for bugs. Happy that they were not being overheard, she leant across the desk towards the interviewing panel and whispered: 'How much do you want it to be?'

* Old accountants never die. They just lose their balance.

* Then there was the accountant who told his client sadly: 'I've looked at your figures and I'm afraid I have terrible news. Last year was the best you ever had'.

* What is the definition of an accountant? Someone who solves a problem you didn't know you had in a way you don't understand.

* A guy finishes his meal in a restaurant and realises he's mislaid his wallet, which had a thousand pounds in it. He stood up and announced: 'I'll give a hundred pounds to anyone who returns my wallet and the thousand pounds inside it'. An accountant dining at a nearby table then stands up and says: 'I'll give two hundred and a free dinner'.

* The owner of a tiny backstreet sandwich shop is hauled up before the tax people. The auditor asks the guy to explain how he can possibly have the cheek to claim tax deductions for trips he's taken to Paris, Rome and Tenerife. The owner of the shop shrugs and says: 'We deliver'.

* One of life's ironies! Isn't it funny that nowadays, if somebody pays cash, you worry that their credit's no good.

* An accountancy firm took on a new employee and very soon, the managers became incredibly impressed with his work and brilliantly quick and accurate arithmetic skills. News soon got to his boss, who decided to congratulate the newbie on how impressed everyone was with him. Then the boss asked : 'Where did you train?' The guy smiled and said: 'Yale'. 'Great', the Boss replied, 'and what's your name?' 'It's Yohnson'.

* This year, the tax people landed me with a huge bill. I rang and asked them to have a heart. They said they'd take it.

WOMEN IN ACCOUNTANCY

The modern world of accountancy is packed full of talented and skilled women. But in Britain, they had to put up an almighty fight to even be allowed to practice as accountants, thanks to institutionalised sexism.

In the United Kingdom, the first woman member of the Institute of Chartered Accountants was Mary Harris Smith in 1919 - thirty one years after she first applied.

The Institute continually turned her down for membership, simply because she was a woman. But in 1919, and as a consequence of the sterling work done by women in commerce and industry during the First World War, the Government passed the Sex Disqualification Act, making it illegal for the Institute to bar women from membership. Aged 72, Mary Harris Smith was belatedly appointed an Honorary Fellow.

It took the august body another full five years before they welcomed their second female member, Ethel Watts, this time by examination. But being a woman in what was then a totally male-dominated profession was hard going. Ethel left the company she worked for to set up her own practice in 1925, Homersham and Watts, sick of being treated so poorly. As a woman, she wasn't even allowed to answer the phone.

Though she was now a member of the Institute, she still faced rather more subtle discrimination. Ethel was barred from attending a number of the organisation's dinners and functions, because they were held in clubs and restaurants that did not admit women. Once, when she complained, Ethel was told she would have been welcome at functions if she'd been a waitress!

But the indomitable Ethel eventually got her own back. Responding to the increase in women members, in 1945 she set up the Women's Chartered Accountants Dining Society.

Ethel finally retired from practice in 1961, a true pioneer in the world of accountancy.

By 2010, almost 50 per cent of the UK and USA's accountancy trainee intake was female. But have women finally managed to smash the glass ceiling? Perhaps not. In the West, it's estimated that only 20 per cent of senior management jobs in accounting and finance are held by women. And that statistic suggests that a lot of firms could be losing out.

Because a recent study conducted by Columbia University - Girl Power: Female Participation In Top Management and Firm Performance (2008) - shows that companies who elevate women to senior management positions experience superior economic performance, because of the different skills they bring to the table. So there!

FORTY ESSENTIAL FINANCIAL FACTS

1. There are 191 official currencies worldwide.
2. Three in every 10,000 US currency notes are counterfeit.
3. The Pound Sterling is the fourth most traded currency in the foreign exchange market, after the US Dollar, The Euro and the Japanese Yen.
4. The world's first credit card was launched in 1951 by American Express.
5. For a good few years, Walt Disney was an accountant's nightmare. In 1921, he founded his first company Laugh-O-Gram- Corp with $15,000 borrowed from investors. Two years later, he was declared bankrupt and completely on his uppers. His next company fared rather better...
6. The IRS employees' tax manual contains detailed instructions on how to collect taxes after a nuclear war.
7. Siberia once used solid blocks of tea as official currency.
8. There are over one million chartered accountants in the USA.
9. The Chinese invented the abacus in around 3000 B.C.
10. Here's something to aspire to! In the USA, Ohio State University is home to the Accountancy Hall of Fame. It honours accountants who have made significant contributions to the

advancement of accountancy. The present Hall of Fame contains esteemed practitioners from the USA, UK, Australia, Canada, Japan and Mexico.

11. Between 1118 and 1307, The Knights Templars used a cheque system to provide their pilgrims with funds. They operated much like our modern day travellers' cheques.

12. You wouldn't want this loose change in your pocket! One million dollars worth of one cent coins weighs 246 tons.

13. Better to fill a suitcase with a million dollars worth of $100 bills, which only weighs in at 22lbs.

14. The world's first mechanical adding machine was invented in the US by Door Eugene Felt in 1887.

15. At the time of the American Civil War, one third of all currency in circulation was counterfeit.

16. Britain's oldest merchant bank, Barings, was founded in 1762.

17. Charles Dickens father, John, was sent to Marshalsea Debtors' Prison in 1824, for a debt of £40 and 10 shillings.

18. The study of currency and the history of money is known as Numismatics.

19. There are currently over four billion $1 dollar bills in public circulation.

20. There are 118 grooves on a dime coin.

21. The Pound Sterling is the world's oldest currency still in use.

22. The first universally accepted banknotes were issued by the Bank of England in 1694.
23. The Bank of Scotland issued their first official banknotes a year later in 1695.
24. Between 1793-1861, around 1,600 private US state banks were allowed to issue and circulate their own money.
25. At the outbreak of World War One, Great Britain had the world's strongest ever economy, holding 40 per cent of the Earth's overseas investments.
26. The USA was the first country in the world to adopt the decimal system for money.
27. Because of strong pressure on the exchange rate for the pound against the dollar, from 1966 until 1977 British tourists were banned from taking more than £50 out of the country.
28. Henry Ford was no big fan of accountants. Though he amassed one of the world's biggest ever fortunes, his company was never audited during his lifetime.
29. The oldest family business in the world is Japan's Houshi Ryokan hotel, which spans 46 generations back to AD 717.
30. To recoup costs incurred from fighting World War Two, in 1945 the USA's top earners were taxed at 94 per cent of their salaries.
31. Britain's first National Lottery tickets went on sale on 14 November, 1994.

32. In 1995, Californian art collector Eli Broad bought a Roy Lichtenstein painting at auction for $2.9 millions. He paid for it on his American Express card, earning himself a dizzying 2.5 million air miles into the bargain. That's enough to circumnavigate the globe 98 times, or make 5 journeys to the Moon and back.
33. The smallest official national banknote ever issued hit the streets of Romania in 1917. The 10 bani note measured just 1.08 x 1.49 ins - about one tenth the size of an American one dollar bill.
34. Paper currency was first issued during the Song dynasty (960-1279) in China.
35. Swiss franc notes are the hardest in the world to counterfeit, containing 18 different security features.
36. The British Tax Year is the only one in the world to run from April 6 to April 5.
37. In terms of money donated to good causes, the most charitable town in Britain is Sunderland. It's also one of the country's poorest communities.
38. In 1953, IBM unveiled the 702, the first business computer.
39. The financial sector is the world's safest job area, with only a 1 in 100 chance of a non-fatal injury or illness.
40. In Kitty Hawk, North Carolina, USA, there is an accountancy firm called 'Scrooge and Marley'.

THE FIRST FINANCIAL SELF-PUBLICIST?

The first official one dollar bill was introduced in 1861-62. At the time, Abraham Lincoln was President of the Union, so you might have expected to maybe see his face on America's first paper currency. If not Lincoln, then perhaps a prominent general, inventor or important historical figure? But no, the man who featured on the first ever one dollar bill was none other than the marvellously named Salmon P. Chase.

A politician, lawyer and avid supporter of the abolition of slavery, Chase became famous for acting as defence attorney for a number of escaped slaves. In 1861, Lincoln appointed him as Secretary of the Treasury at a time when America was riven by Civil War. It fell to Chase to establish a national banking system and the issue of the USA's first legal paper currency.

Though a fine, principled man, Chase's Achilles Heel was an insatiable desire for supreme office. In a brilliant example of self-publicity, he reasoned that putting his own face on dollar bills was a great way for Americans to learn who he was. As it was his responsibility to design the currency, no-one was going to argue with him.

In 1864, he was appointed Chief Justice of the United States; a post he held 'til his death in 1873.

THE BIGGEST AUDIT EVER?

It happened nearly 1000 years ago and involved over 500 'auditors' travelling the length and breadth of England on horse, cart and donkey. It was of course, The Domesday Book and in an age when it took over a week to travel from London to Manchester, was compiled at amazing speed. Begun in 1085, it was completed in the following year.

The "great accounting" was launched by William the Conqueror to discover the exact resources and taxable values of all the manors and boroughs in his new kingdom. He wanted to discover who owned what, how much it was worth - and more to the point, how much was owed to him. Many historians regard The Domesday Book as the first written tax document.

It was by no means a comprehensive audit of England. Important cities such as London and Bristol were not surveyed, partly because they were just too populous and complicated to audit for the manpower the King had available to him. But in total, 13,418 settlements south of the Rivers Ribble and Tees were audited.

The aim? To catalogue the number of serfs, slaves and peasants that each manor or borough contained, as well as the amount of ploughs, livestock, woodland, meadows, pastures, fisheries and mills.

The findings offer a fascinating snapshot of life in 11th century England. What is clear is that the nation was driven by a well-organised agricultural economy. Sixty per cent of the land was being used for arable farming and as pasture and meadow for livestock.

The Domesday Book identified over six thousand water mills that were used to grind grain for bread, and just how dependent communities were on fishing as a food source.
The Book revealed that just one small millpond at Stratford in Warwickshire produced over 1,000 eels per year.

It was a remarkable undertaking and a note in The Domesday Book itself observed: 'There was no single hide nor a yard of land, nor indeed one ox nor one cow nor one pig which was there left out'.

Collated and written up by Royal scribes in Latin, with a few vernacular Anglo Saxon words included, The Domesday Book ran to 913 pages and over two million words.

TEN GREAT SONGS ABOUT MONEY AND ACCOUNTANCY

TAXMAN by The Beatles

Allegedly written by an aghast George Harrison, after being shown how much tax he owed the Inland Revenue by his accountant.

MONEY by The Flying Lizards

If you're going to be one hit wonders, you might as well do it in style. Written by soul supremo Barrett Strong, this Flying Lizard's cover version has been used regularly in films, television dramas and commercials.

FUNKY DOLLAR BILL by George Clinton and Funkadelic

Funky soul madness, taken from the gloriously entitled 1970 album, 'Free Your Mind...And Your Ass Will Follow'.

ACCOUNTANCY SHANTY by Monty Python

The Python team just loved accountants! This classic features in the movie 'The Meaning of Life', and was written by Eric Idle in the style of a 19th century sea shanty. It extols the virtues of all things accountancy. But not very reverently.

CAN'T BUY ME LOVE by The Beatles

Mmm, what money can't buy? Best ask Sir Paul McCartney. A mega hit for The Beatles in 1964, topping both the US and UK charts.

MONEY, MONEY, MONEY by Abba

Though a fairly cynical lyric about the evils of money, ironically this made Agnetha, Anna, Benny and Bjorn an absolute packet. A number one in dozens of countries, it also features in plenty of film soundtracks, including the highest grossing musical film worldwide 'Mamma Mia'.

MONEY by Pink Floyd

Track Six on one of the best-selling albums of all time, Dark Side of the Moon, this paean to the evil of greed allegedly began life in a shed at the bottom of its songwriter Roger Waters' garden.

AFTER TAXES by Johnny Cash

The late, great Man in Black was always on the side of the working man and woman. This is an elegy to what ordinary folks MIGHT have been able to afford - the odd holiday, trinket or treat - if their taxes hadn't been so high.

'THE IRS: WHO'LL PAY FOR MY MEMORIES?'
by Willie Nelson

Not just a song, but a whole album. In 1990, the IRS handed the country and western great a bill for $16.7 million in unpaid taxes and seized most of his assets. In an impassioned effort to free himself from the claim, Willy put out this album to send all profits to the IRS. It worked, and sold in shedloads.

EXECUTIVE COMP by The Accountants

There's no way I couldn't include a song from this mighty band. It's a coruscating number about the obscene perks that bosses bleed out of the system and how they treat their minions with undisguised contempt.

NEVER JUDGE A BOOK BY ITS COVER

In the Swedish coastal town of Skelleftia, Curt Degerman was a familiar sight. Always dressed in a dirty blue jacket and frayed, patched up trousers, locals became used to seeing him pedal his ancient bike around the town's fast food dumpsters and rubbish bins, scavenging for food scraps, and bottles and tins to sell on for recycling to earn himself some cash.

He died of a heart attack in 2008, aged 60. After his funeral, the people of Skelleftia were shocked to discover that the seemingly messed-up bum on the bike had actually been a financial genius.

Spending countless hours in the library poring over the financial newspapers, Degerman taught himself how to play the stock market. Using the little money he earned from collecting tins and bottles, the town tramp became one of the world's shrewdest investors. Using his meagre financial resources, he managed to amass a portfolio of shares worth more than £700,000 - and all from recycled bottles and tins.

Watching dips in the market, he then decided to invest in gold. When he died, his portfolio also included £250,000 worth of gold bars. In addition, he'd bought his house outright, had £4,000 in a personal bank account and £270 in loose change in his home.

And this guy was the crazy bum on the bike...

BAD AT MATHS?

Do you have a friend who's just terrible at Maths? Or indeed, a client? There may well be a real medical neurological reason for this - one that's acknowledged as a problem around the globe by the World Health Organisation.

Dyscalculia is a form of number blindness. It's estimated that between 3-6 percent of the population have the condition. Or put another way, somewhere between 216 and 390 million worldwide. Though regarded as a learning disability the condition occurs in people right across the I.Q. range.

Sufferers often finding difficulty in relating the symbol for a number, say 7, with the actual number of objects that symbol represents. This leads to problems with adding and counting, the knock on effect of which is that sufferers often have difficulties with a whole host of ordinary day to day activities.

Dyscalculars have problems with left/right disorientation, telling the time, understanding rules in games, checking change, budgeting and activities that require sequential processing such as dance steps and reading.

There is currently no known cure, but different learning strategies can be used to alleviate the effects of the condition.

THE BILLIONAIRE WHO ISN'T...

Most people have heard of Bill and Melinda Gates' philanthropic works - but there is another American billionaire who is aiming to give away $8 billion dollars by the year 2016.

Charles 'Chuck' Feeney is an Irish-American Korean War veteran, who first made his fortune selling duty-free liquor to servicemen. He co-founded the Duty Free Shoppers Group and when it sold in the early 1980s, Feeney's share was a cool £8 billion dollars. But the last thing he wanted to do was sit on his fortune.

He made modest provision for himself and his family, then set about giving the rest away, through his Atlantic Philanthropies organisation. To date, he has donated over $4 billion dollars to causes around the world, including over £580 million dollars to his old university, Cornell. Feeney has given $1 billion dollars to education in Ireland and over $220 million to causes in Vietnam.

Feeney's strong belief is: "You should use your wealth to help people". But despite giving away his billions, he won't even allow the smallest plaque identifying him as a donor.

Now in his late seventies, Feeney has instructed the board of his organisation to give away every single dollar it possesses by 2016.

GOOD QUEEN LIZ

Queen Elizabeth II has graced the banknotes of more countries than any other individual in history. Thirty three nations have featured her on their currency, including Australia, New Zealand, Belize, Gibraltar, St Helena, the Falkland Islands, Zimbabwe, Jersey, Guernsey, Malta, Mauritius and Trinidad and Tobago. But curiously, Great Britain wasn't the first!

Seventeen years before Elizabeth became Queen, Canada featured the then nine-year-old Princess Elizabeth on its 1935 $20 note.

During the ensuing 70 or so years, twenty six different portraits of Queen Elizabeth II have been used on banknotes in the UK and its various territories and former colonies. Most countries try to update their currencies to reflect the queen's advancing age. And most countries have featured Her Royal Highness in formal crown and sceptre attire. But the more laidback and nascently republican Aussies and Canadians show her in a plain dress and a string of pearls.

TOP UK MONEY FACT!

Sterling was first introduced as the English currency in 1158 by King Henry II.

Printed in Great Britain
by Amazon